First published in 2017 by Wayland
Copyright © Wayland 2017

Wayland
Carmelite House
50 Victoria Embankment
London EC4Y 0DZ

Managing editor: Victoria Brooker
Creative design: Paul Cherrill

ISBN: 978 0 7502 9955 8

Printed in China

MIX
Paper from
responsible sources
FSC
www.fsc.org
FSC® C104740

Wayland is a division of
Hachette Children's Books,
an Hachette UK company.

www.hachette.co.uk

# THE AMAZING
# LIFE CYCLE OF
# BUTTERFLIES

Written by
Kay Barnham

Illustrated by
Maddie Frost

WAYLAND

In the warmer months of spring and summer, butterflies flutter about. These beautiful insects carry pollen from flower to flower, just like bees.

But did you know that this is just one stage of a butterfly's incredible life cycle?

A butterfly begins its
life as a tiny egg. Some eggs
are round, some are oval
and some are ridged.

The female butterfly sticks her eggs onto leaves or stems, very close together. This plant will soon become food.

Inside the butterfly eggs,
new life is growing. But these
creatures are not yet butterflies.
After a few days, the eggs hatch
and butterfly larvae
appear.

Butterfly larvae are also known as
pupae or caterpillars. At first, they
look like small, wriggling worms.

A caterpillar's job is to eat.
Most caterpillars eat plants,
but some eat other insects.

They eat so much that soon
their skin becomes too tight.
It splits and underneath
is a new, bigger skin.
As the caterpillar grows,
this happens again and again.

Caterpillars have many enemies.
They are gobbled up by birds,
wasps and ladybirds.
In some countries, humans eat them too.

Caterpillars use bristles,
spikes, smells and poison
to frighten away enemies.
Sometimes, they disguise themselves
with eyespots and patterns.

This caterpillar is
pretending to be a snake!

When the caterpillar has finished growing, it hangs upside-down from a leaf or twig. Very slowly, a shell forms around it. This shell is called a chrysalis.

Like the caterpillar, the chrysalis is patterned.
This makes it difficult for enemies to spot.

Inside the chrysalis, something amazing happens. The caterpillar dissolves into a soupy mixture. Then eyes, legs, wings, antennae and other body parts begin to form.

After a week or two,
the caterpillar will have changed
into a brand-new butterfly.

At last, the adult
butterfly pushes its way out
of the chrysalis. This splits open
and the butterfly appears.

It's a tight squeeze inside
the chrysalis. So the butterfly must first
unfold soft wings, which will take
a few hours to harden. Then it
flies for the very first time.

A butterfly has four wings. These are covered with millions of tiny, coloured scales, which make up different patterns.

Some wing patterns
allow butterflies to hide.
Others have special markings
that look like big eyes to scare
away enemies. Bold, bright
colours attract mates.

A butterfly tastes with its feet and smells with
its antennae. Its mouth is shaped like a long tube.
The butterfly uses this to feed on nectar from flowers.

Butterflies can only fly if they are warm.
When they are too cold, they bask in the sun
until their temperature rises.

Some species of butterfly, like the Monarch, live for a few months. But most live for just one or two weeks.

During their short
lives, butterflies mate.
And when the female
butterfly lays eggs,
the life cycle starts
all over again!

Did you know that butterflies are
in danger? Pesticides cause them harm.
And there are fewer wildlife areas for them
to visit. Soon, many species may become extinct.

You can help by planting flowers
such as buddleia, verbena and lavender
in a sunny, sheltered spot. Then wait
for butterflies to appear!

A butterfly's life cycle
has four different stages.
These are egg,
caterpillar, chrysalis
and adult butterfly.

During its life, the butterfly transforms
completely. This amazing process
is called metamorphosis.

# THINGS TO DO

1. A butterfly's wings are covered with many, many scales. Make your own butterfly collage using tiny pieces of coloured paper or tissue to decorate the wings.

2. There is a very long word to describe how a butterfly changes completely during its lifetime: METAMORPHOSIS. How many different words can you make using these letters?

3. Make a butterfly word cloud! Start with 'butterfly' then add any other words this makes you think of. Write them all down using different coloured pens. Start like this...

BUTTERFLY

WINGS CHRYSALIS

# NOTES FOR PARENTS AND TEACHERS

This series aims to encourage children to look at and wonder about different aspects of the world in which they live. Here are more specific ideas for getting more out of this book:

1. Have a butterfly-face-painting competition! Ask children to decorate each others' faces with butterfly designs and then judge the results.

2. Why not decorate a paper plate to show the different stages of a butterfly's life? Then spin the plate to show the life cycle, from butterfly egg to butterfly.

3. There are thousands of different species of butterfly in the world and more are being discovered all the time. Ask children to paint a picture of their own brand-new butterfly and name it.

4. Search online for a time-lapse video of a Monarch caterpillar turning into a chrysalis to show children what this amazing process actually looks like!

# BUTTERFLY BOOKS
# TO SHARE

*Caterpillars and Butterflies*
by Stephanie Turnbull
(Usborne Publishing Ltd, 2006)

*Nature Detective: Butterflies*
by Victoria Munson
(Wayland, 2017)

*Life Cycles: Caterpillar to Butterfly*
by Camilla de la Bédoyère
(QED Publishing, 2010)

*The Great Nature Hunt: Minibeasts*
by Cath Senker
(Frankin Watts, 2016)

*The Very Hungry Caterpillar*
written and illustrated by Eric Carle
(Puffin, 2002)